The Old Scots Surnames

SECRETS AND ORIGINS
OF YOUR NAME

INTRODUCTION

How did we all get surnames? What names come from places? Why was it necessary to distinguish between residents of East Coast fishing villages with the use of nicknames like Snipe, Snuffers, Toothie and Biggelugs? Where do Mr. Hills, Mrs. Craigs and Miss Woods come from?

The answers to these and many other questions about the most important part of your identity are contained in "The Old Scots Surnames," another Lang Syne antiquarian reprint which is presented as a companion volume to "The Old Scots Tongue" and "Strange Old Scots Customs and Superstitions."

It gives the meanings to scores of traditional Scottish names and, as in our other books, there is an outstanding collection of prints showing country life in days gone by.

Acknowledgement

The book was originally published by Edmonston and Douglas, Edinburgh, in 1860 under the title "Concerning Some Scotch Surnames". Through time this leading 19th century publishing house came to be swallowed up by the John Menzies organisation. We would like to thank Mr. W.S. Douglas for his assistance which helped make this facsimile re-print possible.

Historic prints reproduced by courtesy of Edinburgh Libraries.

ISBN 0 946264 13 9

Concerning

Some Scotch Surnames.

NOW that we all have Surnames, we are apt to forget that it was not always so. We cannot easily realise the time when John, Thomas and Andrew, Mary and Abigail, were each satisfied with a single name, nor reflect that the use of two is not a refinement dating from an obscure and unknown antiquity, but quite within the reach of record and history.

Family Names in general.

The Normans are thought to have been the first to introduce the practice of fixed surnames among us; and certainly a little while before the Conquest, some of those adventurers had taken family names from their chateaux in Normandy. "Neither is there any village in Normandy," says Camden, "that gave not denomination to some family in England." But that these Norman surnames had not been of long standing is very certain, for at the Conquest it was only 160 years since the first band of Northmen rowed up the Seine, under their leader Hrolf, whom our history books honour with the theatrical name of Rollo, but who was known among his people as "Hrolf the Ganger."

Used in France A.D. 1000; *in England,* A.D. 1060; *here,* C. 1100.

But whether in imitation of the Norman lords, or from the great convenience of the distinction, the use of fixed surnames arose in France about the year 1000, came into England sixty years later, or with the Norman Conquest, and reached us in Scotland, speaking roundly, about the year 1100.

The first examples of fixed surnames in any number in England, are to be found in the Conqueror's Valuation Book called Domesday. "Yet in England," again to quote the judicious Master Camden, "certain it is, that as the better sort, even from the Conquest, by little and little took surnames, so they were not settled among the common people fully until about the time of Edward the Second."

We had our share of those dashing Norman adventurers who introduced among us the customs of chivalry and the surnames they had adopted from their paternal castles across the Channel. They made a rage for knighthood in both ends of our island, and turned the ladies' heads. An English princess declined to marry a suitor who "had not two names;"* and here in Scotland they became the favourites and companions of our sovereigns; witness the courtiers who surrounded David I. and his grand-sons, whose names—*Brus,* and *Balliol, De Morevil, De Umphravil, De Berkelai, De Quinci, De Vipont, De Vaux,* and a hundred others—still thrill on our tongues, and bring up stories of knightly feats of arms, of the battle-field, and the tilting-ground.

Territorial Surnames.

On the Continent, especially in France, this style of surname, showing its territorial origin—especially where marked by the *De,* so much valued

* Henry I. wished to marry his natural son Robert to Mabel, one of the heiresses of Fitz-Hamon. The lady demurred,—

> " It were to me a great shame
> To have a lord withouten his twa name."
>
> *Robert of Gloster.*

"Whereupon," says Camden, "the King, his father, gave him the name of Fitzroy, who after was Earl of Glocester, and the only worthy of his age in England." Our Countess of Carrick, who laid violent hands on Sir Robert de Bruce, and married him, must have been of the same mind with Mabel Fitz-Hamon.

by our neighbours—is considered as almost the absolute test of *gentry;* and many a pretty French-woman has given herself and her fortune in exchange for little more than the empty sound of the aristocratic prefix. With us it has never been so; and our difference is not merely of language. We have never recognized the principle of raising these territorial names into an aristocracy of gentry—a top cream of society. We have no higher names in England—not even *De Vere, Clifford,* or *Nevil*—than our *Spensers, Fitzgeralds, Stuarts, Butlers,* names which cannot have a territorial origin.

Their Era fixed.

The era of fixed surnames does not rest only on the authority of Camden. It can be proved by a thousand records, English and Scotch. It seems to me it is almost sufficiently proved, when we can show the race of *Stuart*—already first of Scotch families in opulence and power—distinguished by no surnames for several generations after the Norman conquest.* Much later, the ancestors of the princely line of *Hamilton* were known as Walter

* *Alanus dapifer*, whom we now know (thanks to George Chalmers) to have been a son of the great Norman family of Fitz-Alan, was content to distinguish himself in Scotland by the addition of his office alone. His son styled himself Walter Fitz-Alan, and Walter's son was called Alan Fitz-Walter, with the addition of

Fitz-Gilbert, and Gilbert Fitz-Walter, before it occurred to them to assume the name their kinsmen had borne in England. But you must allow me here, and for the present, to rest it on my mere assertion, that surnames were first used among us in the twelfth century, and came into general use in the following one. It disposes of a host of fables in which our forefathers delighted, and some of which were not unworthy of the first decade of Livy.

And so much for the Time.

Lands named before Persons.

As to the derivation of surnames, I beg you to remember, that places were named before families. You have only to examine any of those names which serve for lands and also for persons, to see this plainly. If you found the name of *Cruickshanks,* or *Prettyman, Black-mantle,* or *Great-head,* you would not hesitate. These are evidently coined for persons,

Senescallus Scotiæ—Steward—Stuart—from their hereditary office, which soon became the fixed surname of their descendants.

In like manner, when they complied with the fashion of armorial bearings, which was not till two generations after their settlement in Scotland, they adopted the *fess chequèe* (the *checquer,* used for computing, before the introduction of Arabic numerals), in allusion to their office at the Exchequer table.

and you find no such names of land, or for the double purpose. But then you can have as little doubt that names like *Church-hill, Green-hill, Hazel-wood, Sandilands,* were first given to places; and when you find them borne both by lands and persons, you will conclude the persons took them from the territories. In general, then, when a place and a family have the same name, it is the place that gives name to the people, not the family to the place. This rule, which will not be disputed by any one who has bestowed some study or thought on the subject, has very few exceptions. I may point out some of these afterwards. In the meantime, this enables you to banish, without hesitation, another class of fables, the invention of a set of bungling genealogists, who, by a process like that which heralds call *canting*—catching at a sound—pretend that the *Douglases* had their name from a Gaelic word, said to mean a dark grey man, but which never could be descriptive of a man at all—That the *Forbeses* were at first called *For beast,* because they killed a great bear—That *Dalyell* is from a Gaelic word, meaning, "I dare"—That the *Guthries* were so called from the homely origin of gutting three haddocks for King David the Second's entertainment, when he landed very

Some Fables disposed of.

hungry on the Brae of Bervie from his French voyage.* These clumsy inventions of a late age, if they were really meant to be seriously credited, disappear when we find from record that there were very ancient territories, and even parishes, of Douglas, Forbes, Dalyell, and Guthrie, long before the names came into use as family surnames.†

* In honour of the loyal hospitality of his entertainer, the monarch became poetical, and pronounced

> "*Gut three,*
> Thy name shall be!"

† Hector Boece is answerable for many of these fables. It is he who invented the *Forbes* etymology and the story of the bear. It is he who brought the *homo agrestis* with his two sons and their plough-yokes to stay the rout at Luncarty, and gave them the name of *Hay*, a century or two before our great nobles had surnames. Later authors, with whom goes honest Nisbet, take a bit of Hector's fable and add a circumstance:—The old countryman, after the battle of Luncarty, lying on the ground, wounded and fatigued, cried *Hay! Hay!* "which word became a surname to his posterity."

The old fabler is careful to hang his narratives on popular pegs; and be sure, whenever he makes some prodigious assertion, he quotes "the annals" ostentatiously. Thus, when his visionary Dane King Camus is to be disposed of, he provides him an honourable burial, with the sculptured stones of Aberlemno for a monument. To that local association, he adds the personal one of the origin of one of our most distinguished families. He makes the hero of the field, a gallant youth named *Keth*, *egregius adolescens* Keth *nomine*, UT AB ANNALIBUS TRADITUR; and he then and

Surnames from Normandy.

But passing from these vulgar fables, it cannot be doubted that the great majority of our gentle names are territorial and local. Of those now extant only a few are the surnames imported from Normandy. The names of *Bruce* and *Barclay, Lindsay* and *Sinclair,* indeed, if not so great as they once were, still mark houses of ancestral nobility. But how many have gone down the stream and left no trace! Take the single district of the Border. The *De Vescis,* the *De Morevils,* the *De Viponts, De Normanvils,* the *Avenels,* the *Randolphs*—greater than all, the *De Balliols,* are names now unknown, even in the traditions of Tweedside, where their forefathers ruled as princes. I fear it is against Mr. Aytoun's theory of the high antiquity of

there bestows on him the lands in Lothian, which did, in truth, some centuries later, give name to the family of *Keith* Marischal. In the same way he plays with the name of *Scrimgeour*; and invents a fancy pedigree for the *Stuarts.* The story of Graimus (the ancestor of the *Grahams*) breaking through the Roman wall, he gives on the authority of his great ally Veremund—UTI VEREMUNDUS PRODIDIT. It is the same with places and whole countries, as Buchan, where he deals in Gaelic etymons—Ross, which he derives from certain Irish soldiers called Rosii, who helped to resist the Romans—Caithness, from *Cathus, insignis populi dux* of the same age—all without foundation in chronicle or tradition, and contrary to probability and reason.

our extant ballads, that these names are not found in them. Only the *De Sulis's* have had the fortune of being sung in Border minstrelsy, where they are not represented amiably, being of the unpopular, indeed, unpatriotic faction. The other names have either disappeared, or have suffered a change of a curious kind. The grand old Norman name of De Vesci is now *Veitch*. De Vere, once still greater, is with us *Weir*. De Montealto has come through several steps, till it has rested in the respectable but not illustrious name of *Mowat*. De Monte-fixo is *Muschet*. De Vallibus—De Vaux—De Vaus—by the simple blunder of turning a letter upside down, has assumed the shape of *Vans*; while De Belassize, carrying us back to the times of the Crusades, has in our homely mouths degenerated into the less euphonious name of *Belsches*.

Scotch Local Names.

It would seem as if the surnames taken from places at home were of a hardier growth than those Norman appellations which tried a Scotchman's tongue. Our own local names have changed less—indeed hardly at all—from the places that gave them birth. The *Morays, Crawfurds,* and *Cunninghames,* the *Dunbars, Homes,* and *Dundases,* the *Wemyss's* and *Moncrieffs,* can still point, without hesitation, to the castles or lordships from whence they had their surnames.*

Habitats of Names.

It would be useful, but beyond my present purpose, to give the localities of our more noted names. You must not hope to find them confined to the district where they took their birth. The *Campbells*, to be sure, who first settled in Argyll, still predominate there; but a name almost as great, that of *Gordon*, has left no trace in their native Merse, while they have colonized the northern shire of Aberdeen, rising upon the ruins of the ancient race of *Strathbolgy*. The *De Moravias* (*Murrays*), at one time the great lords of Moray, have scattered into Sutherland and Perthshire, and left no landed man of their name in the province where they once ruled; and so with many others. The *Sinclairs* are still in Caithness, their ancient Earldom; the *Rosses* in the county which gave them their name; but the *Burnetts* and *Irvines* on Dee-side, the *Frasers* in the Aird, and the *Chisholmes*, their neighbours, all transplanted from the south, have thriven more vigorously in their beautiful northern glens. Scott has given us a rhyme that assigns wide bounds for the *Kenne-*

* See some lists of territorial surnames of Scotch families in the Appendix.

*dies,** who, I think, were at first bailies of the great Earls of Carric. The *Grahams* of the Debateable Land, the Annandale *Johnstons,* the *Elliots* and *Armstrongs* on the East Marches, the *Scotts,* and the *Kerrs,* have only changed their peel towers of fence into palaces, and cultivate the valleys where their moss-trooping fathers lived on

> " the good old plan
> That they should take that have the power,
> And they should keep who can."

I am not sure but the middle and lower classes of the agricultural population are more stationary in or about their hereditary settlements than the lords of the soil; but we have not so good means of testing the permanency of their names.†

Though the majority of our ancient family names are territorial, we have many large classes of excep-

* Scott's memory had played him somewhat false. The distich in the earliest shape we have it, and which was undoubtedly his original, runs—

> 'Twixt Wigtoune and the town of Aire,
> And laigh down by the cruives of Cree;
> You shall not get a lodging there,
> Except ye court wi' Kennedy.

† A list of all the parishioners of the parish of Leochel on Donside, who voted in the election of a parish clerk in 1524, is preserved. The minister finds all their names still in the parish in 1860, excepting one or two only.—*Teste Jos. Robertson.*

tions, and the origin of most of them is not doubtful. I have said that surnames came into pretty general use among us in the twelfth and thirteenth centuries. I wish you would turn back with me through the few intervening centuries, and fancy yourselves dwelling in a Scotch town in the time of King William the Lion, or his son Alexander II. The place to which you will be pleased to bear me company is a little burgh by the sea-shore, and where a river's mouth gives shelter to a few rude fishing boats, and one or two barks of larger size, whose decks and taller masts shew them to be seagoing craft, native *busses*, or *farcosts* of Bruges or Antwerp, unloading wine and fine cloths, and waiting for a return cargo of Scotch wool and hides, with some barrels of salmon. Our fancy burgh consists but of one straggling street, leading from the little haven up to the ditch and drawbridge of a turreted castle, which the King has built for the protection of his burgesses, whom he greatly cherishes. The houses of the burghers are low, but built of stone, with tall gables to the street, thatched and warm.

Scotch Burgh of the thirteenth century.

Half way up the street, and with a little space around it, stands the small squat church which has been lately built, of stone, after the new fashion.

Not far from the church is the town hall, where the burghers meet to take counsel; the cross, for royal and burghal solemnities; the tron, or weigh-house; the tolbooth, where toll and custom dues are taken; the jail and stocks, for repressing the contumacious rather than for punishment, which was summary. Beside the river stand mills of more than one kind, some for corn, others for dressing cloth and skins, driven by the stream by means of a simple machinery.

Well, we must not pause longer upon the buildings. Who dwell in this little Scotch "Fair-port" of the thirteenth century? I don't ask their pedigree. It is mixed enough; but all show the stalwart limbs, fair complexion, open countenance of the northern peoples. There are Scots and Picts, Britons and Saxons, Angles and Danes, now mixed together, and rapidly adopting a common tongue, which is one day to speak good sense, not without some music, over half the world. What are they doing, these burghers? Much to the same purpose as their descendants of our times. They plough, and sow, and reap, and bake, and brew. They spin, with rock and distaff, it is true, not with the spinning-jenny, and weave, and stitch their coarse cloth into coarse clothes.

They buy and sell, too, though in a small way. Depend upon it, they love and hate, and marry, and fight, and die and are buried, just like ourselves.

Inhabitants, how named.

Now, in all these acts and events of their little lives, how are our burghers distinguished from each other? Remember, at the time of our visit, fixed surnames—what we call family names—do not yet exist. Each man and woman has only the name given at baptism, and these are not numerous enough to serve the purpose of a growing society. The apostles' and New Testament names, and those of the favourite personages of the Old, are soon exhausted. The known saints and martyrs of the Church come to an end too. The men of the north have a hankering after their old heathenism, and have named their boys and girls after the heroes and heroic ladies of their mythology. Still, population and transactions increase rapidly; and numbers bearing the names of John and James, Andrew and Thomas, Thor, Oggu, and Leysing, Orm, Grim, and Grimketil—jostle each other most inconveniently, and compel the adoption of a remedy. What is it to be? The territorial fashion of the Norman and Saxon lords, who form the rural gentry around them, does not suit them, for they have not much concern with land—at least not as proprietors. But numerous methods offer, when the necessity of the thing becomes manifest.

From Country.

Among the foremost of our townsmen are foreigners or travelled Scots. These take the names of *English,* now written *Inglis, Fleming, French, Welsh* (an epithet which is recognized in its Latin shape of *Wallensis,* and gives rise to the illustrious name of *Wallace*). Some bear the surname of *Ireland,* and even of *Cornwall.* Oddly, some of our people who have wandered into England, return among us bearing the name of *Scott,* which had been given them there. Most of these are moss-troopers on the Border, not addicted to letters; but one has already gone beyond his age in science, and earned the reputation of a warlock. In after years they are to produce a greater wizard.*

Personal Qualities—size.

Next, there is the distinction of size—John *Mickle,* and John *Little,* or John *Small; More* and *Beg* in Gaelic, but I presume only personal appellations, not family names, till some Highlander so distinguished for personal qualities came to settle among the sur-

* Michael Scott, the wizard of Balwearie, was knighted by Alexander III. five hundred years and more before the Lay of the Last Minstrel was published.

named Saxons, and left his name to descendants not all of his own stature. Need I tell you that we have still *Micklejohns* of the size of ordinary mortals; and that *Littlejohn,* who once hunted with Robin Hood in Sherwood Forest, now bakes excellent pies in Leith Street. A Northman who was the first colonizer of Ednam in the Merse, was named Thor. His seal, to be seen in Mr. H. Laing's shop, represents Thor himself seated, with his good sword on his knees, and, lest the likeness should be doubted, the legend around is—*Thor me mittit amico.* But another Thor had the lands of Tranent in this shire. So to distinguish himself, the Merse man calls himself—even in charters and most formal writs—Thor Longus,—Thor the *Long.* The *Longs* were good men in England, as you may read in Clarendon, but not better than the *Langs* and *Laings* of Scotland.

Colours.

Then we have the colours—the families of *Blacks* and *Blackies, Whites,* and *Whytocks* (*Dow* or *Duff* and *Bain,* in Gaelic), *Greys, Browns, Reds* (*Reids, Ruddimans*), *Greens. Blue* is rare, and no man chooses to be yellow.

Stark, and *Stout,* and *Strong,* and *Strang,** and

* The Strangs of Balcaskie, in Fife, had sent an offshoot into Orkney, which produced our first Scotch engraver. He thought fit to do his name into English, and became Sir Robert *Strange.*

Jolly, tell their own history, and we have no difficulty in understanding how they become hereditary. Some names expressing disagreeable qualities are more difficult to understand, since at the period of assuming fixed surnames, the individual ought to have had a vote in applying his own appellation.*

Fisher to-names.

* Our east coast fisher-towns are dependent upon to-names (*agnomina*) for distinguishing individuals. A very curious paper in Blackwood's Magazine (March 1842—why are there no such papers now?) among other peculiarities of the "Fisher folk," gives the following:—

"The fishers are generally in want of surnames . . . There are seldom more than two or three surnames in a fish-town. There are twenty-five George Cowies in Buckie [Cowie is the name of an ancient fishing-village]. The grocers in 'booking' their fisher customers, invariably insert the nick-name or *tee*-name, and, in the case of married men, write down the wife's along with the husband's name. Unmarried debtors have the names of their parents inserted with their own. In the town-register of Peterhead these signatures occur:—Elizabeth Taylor, spouse to John Thomson, *Souples*; Agnes Farquhar, spouse to W. Findlater, *Stouttie*.

. . . . "It is amusing enough to turn over the leaves of a grocer's ledger and see the *tee*-names as they come up:—*Buckie, Beauty, Bam, Biggelugs, Collop, Helldom, the King, the Provost, Rochie, Stoattie, Sillerton, the Smack, Snipe, Snuffers, Toothie, Todlowrie.* Ladies are occasionally found who are gallantly and exquisitely called *the Cutter, the Bear*, etc. Among the twenty-five George Cowies in Buckie there are George Cowie, *doodle*, George Cowie, *carrot*, and George Cowie, *neep*.

"A stranger had occasion to call on a fisherman in one of the

The first *Wiseman* must have stood as high in his own esteem as his eminent namesake of Westminster. *Goodman* and *Goodall* (perhaps *Good-ale*) are also self-complacent names.

I do not find our ancestors named after the Saints

Buchan fishing-villages of the name of Alexander White. Meeting a girl, he asked—

"Could you tell me fa'r Sanny Fite lives?"

"Filk Sanny Fite?"

"Muckle Sanny Fite."

"Filk muckle Sanny Fite?"

"Muckle lang Sanny Fite."

"Filk muckle lang Sanny Fite."

"Muckle lang gleyed Sanny Fite"—shouted the stranger.

"Oh! it's '*Goup-the-Lift*' ye're seeking," cried the girl, "and fat the deevil for, dinna ye speer for the man by his richt name at ance?"

Mr. Forbes Irvine, who directed my attention to this very curious paper, has also supplied the following note from the records of Justiciary. At the Spring Circuit, Aberdeen, in 1844, John Geddes, *alias* "Jock Jack," was indicted for assaulting John Cowie, "*Pum.*"

The *locus delicti* was near the villages of Port-Gordon and Buckie, on the Banffshire coast.

Some of the witnesses were—

Margaret Cowie, "Pum" (daughter of the person assaulted).

John Reid "Joccles."

James Green, "Rovie."

John Geddes, "Jack son."

Alexander Geddes, "Duke."

John Reid, "Dey"—all described as fishermen.

of their birth-days (as in France), but many have names from the season of birth, as *Spring*, *Summer*, *Winter*, *Yule*.

Patronymics.

Another class of distinctive names is the patronymic. Of two Johns one is the Son of John, the other of Thomas, the one becomes John *Johnson*, the other John Thomason or *Thomson*. For a time they fluctuate. Alan the son of Walter had a son Walter, who called himself Walter Alanson, just as, I believe, they do in Shetland to this day.* But gradually the race find it convenient to take a fixed surname from one well-known ancestor. This process gives rise to a large class of surnames, and no doubt very ancient, though the manner of it destroys the proof of sameness of lineage arising from identity of name, as it is evident several Johns and Thomases might give rise to different families bearing the same name. The Norman fashion was to place Fitz (or filius) before the ancestral name, and

At first fluctuating.

Fitz = son.

* I am informed by Lord Neaves, who was formerly Sheriff of Shetland, that within a few years patronymics were very common in those islands, and varied every generation. Thus he used to see produced in the Registration Court titles in favour of Magnus Johnson, whose father was called John Magnus' son (the original of *Manson*), and so alternately for many descents. The women in those families were known only as Mary, John's daughter, etc.

some great families in England and Ireland retain this form, which is also approved for the name of the hero in sentimental novels. But with us, the Norman fashions, like the French language, were of short prevalence. We preferred indicating the descent by the mark of the genitive case, or the affix of the word *Son.* Thus, *Adamson, Adams, Adie,* all mean the same. *Anderson* is the same as *Andrews.* *Richardson, Richards, Dickson, Dickenson, Dick, Dickens, Dickie,* are different ways of expressing the descendants of Richard, whom his friends called affectionately Dick.* So *Johnson, Jones, Jack, Jackson.* So *Davidson,* and *Davy; Rodgers,* and *Hodges,* and *Hodson; Sim, and Simson,* and so through the whole catalogue of names formed upon this principle, which

* It is curious how many of these patronymics are derived from affectionate diminutives as Dickson, Wilson, Watson, Robson, Jackson, Tomson. Is it connected with the practice which, were it not so common, would seem affected, of writing the Christian names in diminutive shape, even in deeds and papers of importance, which was in use chiefly I think about the time when such writings began to be drawn in the vernacular? Wyntoun speaks of "Schir Davy de Lindesay," and of "oure kyng Dawy," but that was perhaps the received shape of the name in our speech. So perhaps we must not judge of the common fashion from the familiar nicknames given in our old family histories, as Wylie Wat, and Christell for Christopher, but we cannot, in such a matter, refuse the authority of the records

are very numerous. Other patronymics are not so obvious in their origin. Pray notice, *Lawson* is not the son of law, or of the lawyer, but of Lawrence, just as the son of Magnus in our northern isles becomes *Manson*. *Laurie* is another shape of Laurenceson, *Kennedy* of Kennethson or *M'Kenzie*.

Of this family, though of later origin, are the Highland patronymics—those which marked descent by the prefix *Mac*, expressing *son*, which continued fluctuating much longer than the *Sons* of the lowlands, and most of which were only fixed into unchanging surnames in the last century. It is understood, I believe, that they assert the descent from some heroic or famous ancestor—a plain advantage over the unpretending Sons of Tom, Dick, and Jenkin. The O of the Irish, literally grandson, and the Ap of the Welsh, in like manner, express abstractly descent.

of Parliament, which give us (*temp. Jac. III.*) "Robin Balmanno," "Sanders Chalmers," etc.; and, in the same reign, we have a process of treason against the Homes and other followers of Alexander Duke of Albany, where the persons indicted under the names "Symonem Salman," and so forth, are *cited* by their ordinary recognized names of Sym Salmon, Will of Leirmont, Pait Diksone "the laird," Dik of Rowlis, Dik of Ethingtonison, Ringan of Wranghame, etc.

Change to Fixed Surnames.

Irish.

In 1465, an Act of the Parliament of Ireland ordained "that every Irishman dwelling betwixt or among Englishmen, in the counties of Dublin, Myeth, Uriel, and Kildare, should go like to one Englishman in apparel, and shaving of his beard above the mouth, should swear allegiance, and should take to him an English surname of *a town*, as Sutton, Chester, Trym, Skryne, Corke, Kinsale; or *colour*, as White, Blacke; or *arte or science*, as Smith or Carpenter; or *office*, as Cooke or Butler, and that he and his issue should use the same."

Welsh.

As to a similar change in Wales, I will take leave to quote Master Camden once more. "In late years, in the time of King Henry VIII., an ancient worshipful gentleman of Wales being called at the pannell of a jury by the name of Thomas Ap William Ap Thomas Ap Richard Ap Hoel Ap Evan Vaghan, etc., was advised by the judge to leave that old manner; whereupon he afterwards called himself Moston, according to the name of his principal house, and left that surname to his posteritie." That was the exception, however; and a more common practice among Welsh families is to take one of their many ancestral names, with a prefix of *Ap*. The *Ap* is sometimes absorbed oddly into the ancestral name;

thus Ap Rice becomes Price; Ap Richard, Pritchard; Ap Owen, Bowen; Ap Hugh, Pugh.

Highland.

Though our Highlanders in their names generally put forward descent of the clan from some heroic or even mythical personage, some tribes have a different manner of surname. The *M'Nabs* (sons of the abbot) seem to have their ancient name as representing the old Abbots of Strathfillan or Glendochart, who had become secularized, and appropriated the lands which belonged to the monastery. Some such descent may be expressed in the name of *M'Pherson,* which means the sons of the parson, *M'Vicar,* and other clerical surnames, as well as in *M'Intosh,* the sons of the chief, and others; while some of the greatest septs, not content with the name recognized among Celts, have another by which they pass in the outer world, as *Cameron, Fraser, Campbell.*

I must leave to more competent hands the curious subject of our Highland and Island surnames, and the endless variety of shapes they assume. I would submit only one or two observations:—

1. The greatest clans were not the earliest to assume uniform fixed surnames, instead of fluctuating patronymics. The Macdonalds and others had

no recognized general surname till almost within the last century. The earliest fixed *Macs* I have met with in record and charter are M'Gilleane (M'Lean), M'Leod, M'Intosh, M'Neill, Mackenzie, M'Dowal, M'Nachtan.

Adoption of Chief's Name.

2. Where the settlement of a powerful southern family within the Highland border is followed by the sudden spread of their name through the neighbouring glens, we may presume—not that the former inhabitants were extirpated, but that the native population (having in truth no surnames) readily adopted that of their new lords. Even after surnames had become common in the Highlands, we find the adoption taking place by written compact. I have seen petitions of some small clans of the Braes of Angus, to be allowed to take the name of *Lyon,* and to be counted clansmen of the Strathmores. Many families and small tribes of Breadalbane in the sixteenth century renounced their natural heads, and took Glenurchy for their chief. Many more, in Argyll and the Isles, must have suffered a change from awe of Maccallummore. The Gordons are hardly settled in the "aucht and forty dauch" of Strathbolgy when the whole country round is full of men calling themselves Gordon.

But this is digression; and I must pray you once more to return to our thriving Scotch burgh of the thirteenth century.

Names from Calling.

Church.

The church, with its establishment, has originated several of our names. Men merely dwelling there are called at Church or of Kirk—shortening, by the common process, into the surnames of *Church* and *Kirk*. *Clerks*, so called from their learning, however they spell their name, are not necessarily in orders, and will leave honourable families descended of them. *Bishop* and *Parson*, *Friar* and *Monk*, are surnames, perhaps marking patronage. *Proctor* is a church officer. *Jore—Dewar—Deuchar*, is curiously connected with the custody of relics. In the choir are *Singers*, *Sangsters* (shortened into *Sang*). Of this class I suppose is the name of *St. Michael*, *Michel*, *Mitchell*, and, of it too, perhaps of the Celtic section of the inhabitants, are men who take the fine names of *Gillies* (servant of Jesus), and *Gilchrist* (Christ's servant) *Gilmichael*, *Gilmory*, or *Gilmour* (servants of St. Michael and Mary), *Gillecalum* and *Malcolm* (servant of Columba), as well as *Gillescop* and *Gillespie* (the Bishop's servant).

Medicine.

The medical profession is represented already. John *Barber* not only trims the beard but breathes a vein, draws a tooth, and performs other surgical offices. His descendant, bearing his name, is to sing the glorious career of Bruce—the Scotch Odyssey. Another practitioner (I suppose he would now be called *physician*), is the Leech. He holds lands and gives service as *Medicus Regis*, the King's Leech, and the surname of him and his family has become fixed as *Leech;* kindred to which is probably the name of *Leechman.*

Trades.

The Merchant Guild has many members. They are in truth the capitalists of our burgh, and have fixed surnames known on the High Street, "where merchants most do congregate." Among these are *Merchant, Mercer* (sometimes *Messer*), *Monypenny, Chapman, Cheape, Seller, Scales, Clinkscales.*

Down at the Mills by the river side there is a busy population. John of the Mill has become John *Mill.* Another has taken the name of *Miller.* The unpopular office of gathering in the multures or mill dues gives the name of Multerer, afterwards to become *Mutter.* *Walkers* are not named from their pedestrian feats, but from the walking or fulling mill where cloth is dressed, which affords the good name of *Fuller* also. The sturdy burgher who put the salmon into barrel for exportation, and also barrels our good home-brewed ale, is known as William *Cooper.* His man who hoops the barrels is John *Girdwood.* The English call him *Hooper.* The officer who stamps the barrels (and I would have you know that the "brand of Aberdeen" passed current through Europe in the fifteenth century), is named the *Brander.* Some of his descendants are people of good account round Elgin at the present day. He is sometimes known as John *Brand* "for shortness;" and we have a respectable colony descended from him, and using that surname, on the coast of Forfarshire.

Beside these worthies in the cooperage is another important trade, that of curing and dressing the skins of our cattle. Here we have people bearing with good right the names of *Barker, Tanner, Currier* (sometimes shortened into *Curry*), and *Skinner.*

You will not doubt that there are, in our thriving community, several *Butchers,* whose name is generally written as well as spoken, *Butchard;* Bakers in plenty, whom we call *Baxters;* makers of ale of both sexes, who think their Scotch name of *Brewster* quite as good as the southern *Brewer;* shoemakers and weavers, in the vernacular, *Suters* and *Websters.* The dyer is with us a *Litster.* The

Southrons have borrowed the name (making it *Lister*) without knowing its meaning. We have in our village, *Cooks, Kitchens* and *Kitcheners, Tailors, Turners, Saddlers, Lorimers* (*i.e.*, bridle makers), *Glovers.* Of workers in wood we have *Wrights* (whom the English call *Carpenter*), *Cartwrights, Sievewrights, Joiners, Sawers.* The old trade-name of *Glasenwright* is to die out, but we have numerous *Masons, Sclaters, Plumbers,* all affording respectable and enduring surnames.

Two important handicrafts at the time of our imaginary visit are soon to disappear, leaving only their names to their posterity. The maker of bows, the chief arm of war, is called *Bowyer* and sometimes *Bowmaker* (one of that family is to be known a century later as Abbot of the Monastery of Inchcolme, and continuator of John of Fordun's Scotch Chronicles). The arrow-makers (whom the French name Flêchier from flêche), are with us known as *Fletchers,* a name that is to survive and flourish long after their good weapons have given way before "the villanous Saltpetre."

Smith.

The chief artisan of the community is the Smith, a stalwart man, whose descendants are to increase and multiply till they replenish the earth. We must not quite take our idea of him from the modern attendant of the forge and anvil, nor even from Longfellow's fine portrait of the village blacksmith—

> "Under a spreading chestnut tree,
> The village smithy stands;
> The smith, a mighty man is he,
> With large and sinewy hands;
> And the muscles of his brawny arms
> Are strong as iron bands.
>
> . . . .
>
> "Toiling—rejoicing—sorrowing,
> Onward through life he goes;
> Each morning sees some task begun,
> Each evening sees it close;
> Something attempted, something done,
> Has earned a night's repose."

Among our forefathers, as among the ancient Greeks, the Smith's was a craft of mystery, if not of magic. Remember, he forged the armour that guarded the heads of warriors, and welded the sword of such temper that it scorned enchantment, cut through iron and brass, and yet severed a hair upon water. In the ancient laws of England, the Smith's person was protected by a double penalty. In Wales he was one of the great officers who sat in the hall with the King and Queen. In our own Highland glens I have heard more legends of supernatural smith-work than ever I could gather of Ossian. We must not wonder, then, that the family of *Smith* is large, nor that it assumes many forms of spelling in our low country talk, as well as the shape of *Gow,* and probably *Cowan,* among those whose mother tongue is Gaelic.*

Minstrels.

Amidst some business and bustle, there is still much leisure in our infant society; and how can the long evenings by the winter fire be better whiled away—when the wine gets sour, and chess and tables tedious—than in rehearsing the deeds of valiant ancestors or the adventures of a pilgrimage or crusade! He who has composed the romance or lay, does not always sing it. The *Bard* and the *Harper* are alike honoured; and both are to leave descendants, though the former may change their spelling for the worse, and both may, I fear, depart from the calling that gave them their surnames.†

* The punctilio of orthography is of very modern date. Our grandfathers, and still more, our grandmothers, used wonderful license, not only with their neighbours' names, but with their own. In the sixteenth century, when writing had become a common accomplishment, a man often spelt his own name six or seven different ways in a single letter. The surname of the Stirlings (of Keir) is found in their family papers, spelt in sixty-four different manners. No wonder that the name of *Smith* should run through the shapes of *Smith, Smyth, Smythe.*

† The historian of an extant family of the ancient name of *Baird,*

The necessity of some distinction before surnames are common, gives rise to a curious custom in our burgh. Men distinguish themselves and their dwellings by signs or cognizances. It is not only inns and shops or booths that exhibit these emblems; burghers and gentry of all classes do the same. This gives us a class of names common to France, England, and Scotland. John at the Bell becomes John *Bell*, and the Lamb, a favourite cognizance, in connection with the symbol of Saint John, originates the family of *Lamb*, and its affectionate diminutive *Lamby*—a name once of good repute as a native name in Angus, though those who bear it in modern times have sought a French origin, and spell it *L'Ami*. The same custom gave rise among our neighbours in the south, to the name of *Angel*, and even the strange one of *Devil*, neither of which we have affected. But we have *Kings* and *Bishops*, and even a few *Popes* in our Presbyterian Scotland—names probably to be traced to a similar origin. A

Names from Signs.

not satisfied with such a probable connection with the Muses, claims for them, kindred with *Boiardo* the Italian poet. But we had *Bairds* or *Bards*, landed men, much earlier than suits that poetic origin. A more tempting etymon from Bayard, *the chevalier sans peur et sans reproche*, had not occurred to the Auchmedden historian.

little clan of these last, pronounced *Paip*, exists in Caithness and Orkney.* I conjecture that the same practice has given origin to many of our names commencing with *Saint*,† and probably it is to this custom that we owe a large class of names that are not otherwise easily to be accounted for—I mean the family names derived from names of animals. Even if we suppose that some accidental relation to the animals suggested the names of *Hare* and *Dog* (which we spell absurdly *Doig*), *Brock*, our Scotch shape of Badger, and the well-known names of *Swan*, *Eagle*, *Heron*, *Peacock*, and *Craw*, we cannot adopt such an origin for the surname of *Oliphant* (the Scotch shape of Elephant), or of *Lion*, the name of the noble family of Strathmore, whose family tradition does not point to any foreign source, but who can hardly allege an encounter with the royal beast in

* Alexander Pope, whose Christian name smacks of a Scotch descent, did not repel the advances of his Caithness namesake, Mr. Paip, who claimed him for kindred. Against the theory in the text, is the fact, that the Norsemen called Christian priests *papas*; and some of the islands are named *Papey* from early settlements of such.

† In a country town of Spain, the booths of the traders are distinguished by oval medallions of saints swinging in front—St. James, St. John, St. Andrew—each known by his received cognizance, but without name inscribed, either of saint or shopkeeper.

the forests of Angus. They bore for their coat armour the Lion of Scotland, and may perhaps have exhibited a lion over their gate, as, we know, they constructed in the shape of a lion that curious silver cup still preserved at Glammis, and which is the prototype of the "blessed bear of Bradwardine."*

But now we have set up our burgh with a good stock of surnames, and we must leave them to increase and multiply, or to decay as it may happen, for I have only time to offer you a few observations upon names which did not originate in burgh or town.

Where names are seeking, people are naturally called by the name of the place where they have been born or live. So you cannot wonder that, in our own dear country, we have many *Hills* and *Glens, Craigs, Woods,* and *Forrests.* *Mountain* is a more English form of *Hill.* We have the hills too near, and like them too well, to give them grand sounding names.

Moors.

The *Moor* has given names to families in all the

* The affixing of cognizances on their houses by citizens, not traders, is well known to the French antiquary. It was common in Spain, and seems to have been often used in England. I have not seen *evidence* of the practice in Scotland, but we were not slow to follow the fashions of our neighbours in such matters.

three kingdoms. With us they have enjoyed our usual license of spelling, but the origin and sense of the word is the same whether it is spelt as the good Sir Thomas *More* used it, or like the Irish Anacreon, Moore, or our antique Scotch *Muir.* I have observed that, in all its shapes, the name connects itself with literature. One of our best Greek scholars of the last century was Professor Moor of Glasgow. Our foremost Grecian now is a Mure.* The author of Zeluco, and his more illustrious son (Sir John Moore) added an *e* to the name "for a difference," and some such cause has produced the various reading, *Moir,* still distinguished for the strong propensity to literature.

Offices.

Of names derived from office, first in this country comes *Stewart,* variously spelt, though, as I have already told you, it was not till after several generations that the Fitz-Walters and Fitz-Alans took that name destined to become so illustrious, from their office of steward of the royal household.

We have names derived from all other offices of

* It must be remembered this was written in 1857. William Mure of Caldwell, the accomplished historian of Greek literature—accomplished in a way so rare among Scotch country gentlemen, died in the spring of 1860.

high and of low degree. The office of keeper of the Wardrobe gave name to a family of *Wardropers,* since shortened into *Wardrop,* just as *Forrester* was cut down into *Forrest.* The keepers of the Napery became *Naperers* (cut down to *Naper*).* The great office of *Ostiar,* or *Durward,* gave name to a powerful family, now extinct or sadly decayed; but, even yet, the Deeside peasant believes that the church bell of Coul rings of its own accord when a Durward dies; and I am inclined to trace another old Angus name to the same source. The Doorward may have become *Huissier,* and Huissier easily took the Scotch shape of *Wischart.*

I beg you to observe that the dignity of the office has no bearing on the grandeur of the family that adopted it for a name. The name of *Sheriff* is by no means higher than that of *Dempster,*† though

* *Nà peer—non pareille*—is the childish etymology of the genealogists for the name rendered illustrious by John Napier of Merchiston, and borne by many a gallant man of our own time.

† The *Dempsters* had their name from their office. Keraldus was hereditary Judex (translated *Dempster*), first of Angus, then of the Court of the Kings of Scotland; and a long line of *Dempsters* held the lands, called from their ancestor Keraldston (now Carriston), in virtue of that office, the duties of which they discharged in Parliament. Judex was perhaps done into *Justice* in the South.

the latter was the mere organ for pronouncing the sentence of the court, while the former was, and still is, a high officer of the Crown. The great office of Chamberlain gave rise to the different shapes of the name of *Chambers,* and *Chalmers,* and *Chamberleyn.* *Constable* is not so high a name with us as in England; but *Baillie* has acquired respect from being borne by some good men and most amiable women. The Memoir of Lady Grizel Baillie (I hope the book is as well known as it deserves to be), is better than a patent of nobility. I must not detain you with other official names. We have *Marshalls* in middle life, and *Porters* quite as high. The first tailor who did me the honour to dress me in man's apparel was a *Chancellor.* Mr. *Laird* is no more dignified than Mr. *Tennent.* The *Gentleman*, the *Knight,* and the *Barron,* are quite on a level.

Rural Occupations.

Rural pursuits and occupations predominate among us. Thus we had *Tennant, Farmer, Grieve,* and *Fairgrieve;** *Carter, Shepherd, Shearer, Har-*

* *Grieve* may have its origin in a higher office; perhaps the Shire-grieve or Sheriff. Beside Elgin, and again near Forres, there are estates called "Greeship Lands," which I take to have been attached to the office of Sheriff when there were sheriffs and courts at each of these burghs.

rower, Tasker, Thrasher, or *Thrashie. Bowman* was the man in charge of the *Bow,* or cattle; *Husband,* he who cultivated the portion of soil which derived from him the name of husband-land, a measure known in the Merse and Lothian. *Granger* has his name from looking after the grange, or homestead of a farm.

We had naturally many names from hunting and the chase. We had no *Grosvenors,* but we have *Tod-hunter,* not quite equivalent to a Leicestershire master of hounds, now shortened into Tod, *Hunter* and *Fischer, Falconer* and *Fowler.* The Falconers called their domain *Halkerston* (Hawker's town), and a family of reputation derived its surname from the town of the Fowler—*Fullerton.* The park-keeper became *Parker,* and the officer in charge of the warren, *Warrener,* or *Warrender,* equivalent to the Norman De Warrenne. The guardian of the forest took many shapes of name—*Forrester, Forster, Foster, Forrest,* and even *Forret.* We have *Archers,* and *Stalkers,* and *Spearmans,* the last speaking perhaps of more warlike occupations.

I have said that the rule of persons being named from places—not places from persons—has a few exceptions. The most remarkable is *Hamilton.*

Hamilton.

We can mark in records the race of Fitz-Gilbert settling down into the fixed surname of *Hamilton,* and, soon afterwards, the piece of land, then called the Orchard, probably a portion of their demesne of Cadyow, acquiring from them the name of Hamilton, which has since attached to the dependent village, as well as to the palace, now richer in noble works of art than any other in Scotland.

Town and Ville.

A much more common way of affixing personal names upon lands was by subjoining the word town or the French *ville* to the family name. The settlers of Teutonic speech took the former; the Normans, who used French, the latter. Thor, Orm, Dodin, and Leving, Edulf and Edmund, known as early settlers in Lothian, have left their names in *Ormiston,* and *Thurston,* and *Duddingston,* and *Livingston, Eddleston* and *Edmonston;* names of places, most of which have again conferred territorial names on extant families.

The Vill of the Norman settler has sometimes among us taken the shape of *well.* Maccus, a personage of large possessions in the reign of David I., seems to have used both modes of denominating his land. One of his places he called Maccustun, now Maxton; another Maccusville, which soon became

Maxwell. Afterwards, his descendants, or at any rate the holders of his lands, took the territorial style of De *Maxwell.* A third step has been taken in this case, by again adding town to the family name and producing Maxwellton. *Boswell* and *Freshwell* are formed in the same manner.

Translated Names.

One word on the confusion occasioned by *translating* names. From the French *Le-fevre* and *Marechal,* have come some additions to our own large clan of *Smiths,* and *De Bois* has given us many *Woods.* We made De la Roche and De Rupe into *Craig.* Two brothers, Frenchmen by descent, but settled in an American town, are even now Mr. De la Rue and Mr. Street. But the change was worse when our scholars made the pedantic attempt to render our homely names classical. The Matriculation book of our Edinburgh University in the seventeenth century is subscribed by a student whom mortals called *Blyth,* but who, aiming at something higher, writes his own name *Hilarius;* while another christened Colin *Caldwell,* subscribes the oaths of admission as Colinus *a fonte gelido.*

This became still more intolerable when the classical affectation adopted a Greek dress. We have almost lost memory of the real name of one of the great leaders of the Reformation, whose paternal name of Schwartzerdt (black earth) has permanently merged in its Greek shape of *Melanchthon;* while another has gone through the double process of translation through Latin into Greek, passing in at one end of the mill as *Didier,* and coming out *Erasmus.* A well-known instance of our own is similar. *Wischart,* the historian of Montrose, chose to read his name as Wise-heart, and then to Helenise it into *Sopho-cardius.*

Irish instances.

Of late years we have changes of a different kind, and from other motives. If you will allow me, I will take my examples from our Irish cousins, whose mixed Celtic population, and some other circumstances not altogether unlike our own, give rise to curious tricks of transmutation. Irish names are translated into English. Thus Shannach is Fox. Mac-Clogh-ree is now Kingstone. But much more common is the Irishing of Norman-English names. Thus a known personage, Joscelin de Angelo (first done into *Nangle*), is succeeded by MacGostelin, which in one or two descents becomes *Costello,* a name now known in literature. Sir Odo the archdeacon had a son Mac-Odo, now vulgarized into

Cody. Sir Waleran Wellesley gave rise to a sept of *Mac-Falrans.*

De Montmorenci.

Of another class is the change (whether founded on evidence it is not for me to pronounce) by which an Irish gentleman of the name of *Morris*, living in Paris, became De Montmorenci, and persuaded his Irish relatives to follow his example. They acquired at least a good name; but the descendants of the *premier baron Chretien* called a council of the family, and published an Act enumerating all those whom they recognized as genuine—in which the Irish cousins were not included.

M'Alpin.

One more story from across the channel. A Dublin citizen (I think a dealer in snuff and tobacco), about the end of last century, had lived to a good age and in good repute, under the name of *Halfpenny.* He throve in trade, and his children prevailed on him in his latter years to change the name which they thought undignified, and this he did by simply dropping the last letter. He died and was buried as Mr. *Halpen.* The fortune of the family did not recede, and the son of our citizen thought proper to renounce retail dealing, and at the same time looked about for a euphonious change of name. He made no scruple of dropping the unnecessary *h*, and that being done, it was easy to go into the Celtic rage, which Sir Walter Scott and the Lady of the Lake had just raised to a great height; and he who had run the streets as little Kenny Halfpenny came out (in full Rob Roy tartan, I trust), at the levees of the day as Kenneth *MacAlpin*, the descendant of a hundred kings.

Conclusion.

But to return and to conclude. In one sense it may be true that the age of chivalry is gone. The high-born knight may no longer put on his armour of proof, and ride down the *jacquerie** unblamed. We look for better things of gentle blood now. But we value it all the more. Without absurdly glorifying ourselves, we have some reason to be proud of our Scotch names. Whilst we give up without a struggle the antiquity claimed for families by our genealogists—whose youngest fable dated from Malcolm Canmore, while there were not wanting some who ascended to Noah—we can boast that we have among us many still bearing the names, and descended of the little band of heroes that fought with Bruce. What is more; I think we can say that while we are alive to the interest of a

* Froissart's name for the peasantry, the class composed of the "*Jacques bon-hommes*."

long descended line of worthy ancestors, as much as our neighbours, we keep that feeling in our hearts and do not blazon it to the world. It never interferes with the transactions and affairs of every-day life. Above all, there is no exclusion of new blood. I suppose the descendants of a James Watt or a Robert Burns would not change the honour of their descent for the highest name of Norman chivalry.

I.—Some SCOTCH SURNAMES derived from Lands in Scotland.

Abercrombie.
Aberdeen.
Abernethy.[1]
Ainslie.
Auchinleck.
Allardice.
Alves.
Anstruther.
Arbuthnot.
Auchmutie.
Aytoun.

Balfour.
Balderston.
Ballindean, Ballantyne, Bannatyne.
Ballingall.
Balneaves, Balnevis (*de villa nativorum*), shortened into Neaves.
Balsillie.
Bassinden.
Berwick.
Binning.
Blacadder.
Blackburn.
Blackhall.
Blackwood.
Blair.
Borland.
Borthwick.
Bog, Boig, Boog.
Boncle.
Briggs, Bridges, like Vipont, Pontif.
Brackenrigg.
Brisbane.
Braidwood, Broadwood.
Brodie.
Brounlie.

[1] One of our noble names derived from ancient church lords. The Abbot, secularising, appropriated the lands, and his descendants took their surname from the benefice.

Brunton.
Buchan.
Buchanan.
Buntine, Bontine.
Burnett, Burnard,
Burton.
Burn, Burns, Burnes, Burness.
Byres.

Calder, Cawdor, Caddell.[1]
Calderwood.
Cairncross.
Callander.
Cameron.
Carkettle.
Carlisle.
Carmichael.
Carnegie.
Carrick.
Carron.
Carruthers.
Carstairs.
Carswell.
Cathcart.
Cheislie.
Chisholme.
Clapperton.
Clayhills.
Cleghorn.
Cleland.
Clephane.
Cochran.
Cockburn.
Colquhoun ?
Colvil, vulgarized Colvin.
Copland.
Cowie.
Craig, Craigie.
Crauford.
Cranstoun.[2]

[1] The northern *Cawdors* were disguised as *Codells* and *de Cadella* even in our old chroniclers, and they have kept that variety permanently in the South. So *Lincoln*, in Norman French, took the shape of *Nicolle*. There are Napiers, in the North, vulgarly called Lepers—*euphoniæ causa!*

[2] We almost forgive the old condemned *canting* arms of our heralds, for the sake of the Cranstoun's crest and motto—a crane fishing—and "Thou shalt want e're I want."

Crichtoun.
Crombie.
Crosbie.
Cullen.
Cuninghame.

Dalgarno.
Dalgleish.
Dalmahoy.
Dalrymple.
Dalyell.
Dean, Dein, Deinis.
Denham, Denholm.
Dennistoun, Danielstoun.
Dingwall.
Dinwoodie.
Dollas, Dallas.
Don.
Douglas.
Downie.
Drummond.
Drysdale, Dryfesdale.
Duffus.[1]
Dunbar.
Dundas.
Dunlop.
Durham.
Durie.
Dykes.

Easton.
Eccles.
Edington.
Edmonston.
Elphinston.
Erskine.

Fairholme.
Fairie, Ferry.
Fairlie.
Fiddes, Futhes, Fuddes.
Fife.
Forbes.
Forrest, Forrester, Foster, Froster.
Forsyth.

[1] The old lordship and castle of the De Moravias, which give name to the people called Duffus, are themselves generally referred to a Gaelic Etymon. In charters older than might be supposed, I find the place written *Dufhus*, suggesting the homely origin of *columbarium* or dove-cot.

Fotheringham.
Foulis.
Fultoun.
Fullarton, (*de villa aucupis*).

Gardyne, Gardiner, Jardine.
Galbraith.
Galloway.
Garioch.
Geddes.
Gifford.
Gladstone, Gledstains.
Glasfuird.
Glendonwyn, Glendinning.
Gourlay.
Govane.
Gordon.
Guthrie.
Graham.
Gray.
Greenhill.
Greenlies.
Grote.

Halket, Halkhead.
Hadden, Halden.
Hagart, Hogarth.
Halçro.
Halkerston (*villa aucupis*, the messuage of the Fauconers).
Hall (*de aula*).
Halyburton.
Hedderwick.
Hepburn.
Heriot.
Herris.
Hislop.
Home, Hume.
Hop-pringle, Pringle.
Horsburgh.
Houstoun (*de villa Hugonis*).
Howburn.
Howden.
Hutton.
Hyndshaw.

Innes.
Irvine.

Jellybrands.
Johnston.

Keir, Kerr, Carr.
Keith.
Kells.
Kennoway.

Kilgour.
Kincaid.
Kincardin.
Kinloch.
Kinnaird.
Kinnear.
Kirkaldie.
Kirko.
Kirkpatrick, Kilpatrick.
Kirkwood.
Knowes, Knox, Knollis.
Kyle.
Kyninmonth.[1]
Laidlaw.

[1] The old bishops of St. Andrews, in the twelfth century, had their great officers named like those of royalty. Odo was the bishop's seneschal; Hugo, pincerna or butler; William, the chamberlain; Gamelin, the doorward; Geoffry, the dapifer; William, the marischal. From that Odo the seneschal, descended a race of Odos and Adams, who held the office hereditarily, and, in progress of time, took the surname of Kininmonth, from the lands attached to their hereditary office. One of their descendants, James of Kinninmond, of that ilk, knight, in 1438, presented a claim of right to certain Fife notables, acting as friendly arbiters between him and the Lord Prior of St. Andrews in these words:—"Rycht worschippfull lord and derast maistir, Jamys of Kyninmond of that ilke, youre humble servand rycht mekly besekis youre hee lordschip, and your worschipfull convent, and youre discrete consale, at the reverence of God, that ye wald do me law and resoune in favorabill manere in thir poynctis: That is to say, that the purtenence that I want of the lordschip of Kyninmond, in the first Monniacky medow, sen I am possessit of part of it, considering that it did yow never proffit. *Item*, sen Ovirmalgask is fundin a tenandry in yowr awin court of the fornemyt lordschip, that I micht have fre recourse therto, with youre emplesance. *Item*, youre bailyery, landsteuartry, marschalry, I clame thir poynctis in fee and heritage, with houshald for me and twa gentilmen, twa

Lamont.
Landels.
Langlands.
Law.
Lawder.
Learmonth.
Leask.
Leith.
Lennox.
Lentron.
Leslie, Lescelin.
Letham.
Lichton, Leighton.
Liddell.
Linkletter.
Linton.
Lithgow.
Livingston (*de villa Levini*).
Lizars (*de Lysuris*), Lesows.
Lockart, Loccard, Lockhart.[1]
Logan.
Logie.
Lothian.
Lumsden.
Lundy, Lundin.
Lyall.
Lympitlaw.
Lyne.

Maine.
Maistertoun.

yemen, with the boyis folowand my wyfe, and twa gentillwomen with hir, with sic houshald as afferis; a falcoune and a goishawk; a braiss of greuhundis, and a coppil of rachis; the best chaumer, the best stabill, next my lordis, with fourty pund of fee folowand thir offices. And in all thir fornemyt poynctis that I micht haf a gracious and a favorabill deliverance, but prejudice, I besek youre hee lordschip and grace at the reverence of God, our Lady and Saynctandrow."

[1] The last spelling has given rise to the "canting" arms of the lock and the heart, and to the myth about the ancestor of the Lockharts securing the Bruce's heart which Douglas perilled in the fight with the Moors.

Maitland, Maltaland.[1]
Manderstoun.
Manfod.
Marjoribanks.
Maxton.
Maxwell.
Meggat.
Meldrum.
Melvil, vulgarized Melvin.[2]
Menzies.[3]
Methven.
Middleton.
Milliken, Milligan.
Motherwell.
Moffat.
Moncrieff.
Moncur.
Monro.[4]
Monteith, Menteath.
Morton.
Moscrop.
Mow, Molle.
Murray, Moray.
Mutray.

Nairn.
Nevay.
Newall.
Newbiggin.
Newton.
Nisbet.
Norie.

Ogill.
Ogilvie.
Ochterlony.
Ogstoun.
Ormiston.

[1] The old pedigree writers have sought a French origin for this name, in *mau talent*, without proof or much probability.

[2] Translated in old charters, *de mala villa*. The name Melvin, on the north-east coast, is pronounced Mellon. Of old there was a family in the North, styled Bonville, *de bona villa*.

[3] I don't know this place, the name is ancient with us, and seems the same with *de maneriis*, Manners.

[4] It is with some doubt that I place the name among Scotch local surnames, though the family has been very long settled in Ferindonald.

Orr.
Orrock.
Osburn.

Pantoun.
Pargillies.
Park.
Patullo.
Peddie, Pepdie.
Peeblis.
Pennycuik.
Pentland.
Pitblado.
Pitcairn.
Pittendreich, Pendrich, Pender?
Plenderleith.
Polloc (Pook).
Pont.
Porterfield.
Preston.
Primrose.
Provan.
Purdie.
Purves.

Rait.
Ray.
Ralstoun.
Randell.
Rankeillor.
Rankin.
Rattray.
Redpeth.
Reidheuch.
Rentoun.
Riddell.
Riddoch.
Rigg.
Rochead.
Rollock, Rollo.
Rolland, Rowane.
Ross.
Roxburgh.
Rule.
Rutherfurd.
Ruthven.
Rynd.

Saintserf, Sydserf.
Sandford.
Sandilands.
Sands.
Sauchie.
Schaw.
Scougall.

Scouler.
Scroggie, Scroggis.
Scrymgeour.
Seaton.
Selkirk.
Sempill.
Sheill.
Shives.
Shoreswood.
Sibbald.
Skene.[1]
Skelton.
Skirling.
Skirving.
Smailholm.
Smeaton.
Smollet.
Snodgras.
Sommervil.
Spalding.
Spittall (*de hospitali*).
Spottiswood.
Spreull.
Stenhouse.
Stirling.
Stobs.
Stodholme.
Strachan.
Stratherne.
Stratoun.
Street.
Struthers.
Suittie, Sutty.
Sutherland.
Swinton.
Symontoun (*de villa Symonis*).

Thorburn, Thorbrand, Thornebrand.
Thorntoun.
Tindall, Tynedal.
Todrig.
Torrance.
Touch.
Touris.
Trail, Troil.
Traquair.
Troupe.

[1] A seal of the Laird of Skene, affixed to the homages, (*temp. Ed. I.*) giving three dirks or *skeens*, shews the antiquity of "canting" arms with us. The name is territorial, the lordship forming the parish of Skene.

Tulliedeff.
Tulloch, Tullos.
Tweedie.
Tynto.
Tyrie.

Uchiltree, Ochiltree.
Udney.
Udward, Uddart.
Urie, Ure.
Urquhart.

Waddell.
Wardlaw.
Walkinshaw.
Wark.
Wauchope.
Wedderburne.
Wemyss.
Whitehead.
Whitelaw.
Whytford.
Winzett.
Winlaw.
Winram.
Wotherspon.
Wood.
Wryttoun.

2.—A few Extant SCOTCH FAMILY NAMES, derived from Places in England or Normandy.

Balliol.[1]
Barclay, de Berkelai.
Bethune, Beton, Beaton.
Boyle.
Bruce, Brus.
Byset, de Byseth, Bisset.[2]

[1] I fear this great name is extinct. Some have supposed it to survive in Baillie.

[2] Lords of Lovat, and of great power in the North as well as in Southern Scotland, before their tragic fall in 1242. They are said to have migrated to Ireland, and to have left descendants there. A branch remains in Aberdeenshire.

Campbell.[1]

Charteris, de Chartreux, *de domo Carthusianorum*, Charter house.

Cheyne, le Chene.[2]

Corbet.[3]

Cumin, Cumming, Comyn.[4]

[1] This name, now so numerous and powerful, first appears on record in the end of the thirteenth century. The earlier history of the family, and the origin of the name, are unknown. It is not local, at least, not derived from any Scotch locality (for Castle Campbell, formerly the 'Castle of Gloom,' took its name from the family in virtue of an Act of Parliament), and I am not aware that the peculiar and very ancient heraldic bearing (the *Giron*) affords any probable theory of connection with Continental or English families. Like all names of families settled in the Highlands, Campbell is claimed by the Seanachies as Celtic, and an etymology and legend are furnished on demand. The appearance of the Campbells (already evidently full-blown gentry), at the same time with numerous Norman settlers; their alliance with the Norman Bruce; the sound and spelling of their name, which seems only another shape of Beauchamp, leave little doubt that it is Norman. It would require some evidence to get over the presumption.

[2] Reginald le Chen, father and son (giving between six cross crosslets a bend charged with three figures, perhaps mullets), early settlers in the North, seem Normans, but the derivation of their name is uncertain, perhaps akin to *Du chesne*.

[3] An old name in the South. Their cognisance was a *Corbeau*.

[4] One of the numerous families ruined by their adherence to the Balliols and the English party in the wars of the succession and independence. Fordun says, before their fall, there were thirty-two knights of that surname in Scotland, including, I presume, the lords of their three great earldoms, Buchan, Badenoch, and Menteth.

Grant, Graunt, le Grand.[1]

Haig.
Hamilton, de Hambledon.[2]
Hay, de la Haye.

Lindsay, de Lindeseye.
Lyle, De l'isle.

Lovel.[3]

Maule.[4]
Montgomery.[5]
Mowbray.[6]
Mortimer, *de mortuo mari.*
Mowat, *de monte alto.*
Muschet, *de monte fixo.*

[1] The first who appear on record are Laurence and Robert, "called Grant"—*Dominis Laurentio et Roberto dictis Grant*—witnesses in the bishop's court A.D. 1258. At a later period the Grants are found settled on the barony of Strathspey as church vassals, until at the Reformation they acquired it in property.

[2] The English (Leicester) pedigree of Hamilton is only guessed. They had been for three generations settled in Scotland before taking any fixed surname. Their power and consequence were of comparatively late date, not, I think, before the royal marriage, by which they acquired the earldom of Arran.

[3] The Lovels were considerable lords in Angus, the North, and on Tweedside, now, I suppose, extinct.

[4] The Maules, themselves Normans, derived their chief possessions from inheriting, through an heiress, the property of the great family of *De Valoniis, de Valoines.*

[5] The Montgomeries, like so many of the Ayrshire and Renfrewshire families, came as followers of the Stuarts. They had grants from them, both in their Lothian territory and in their great western lordships.

[6] No doubt a branch of the great English-Norman family, settled early at Barnbougle, and sent a cadet to the opposite Fife coast.

Muschamps, de Muscamp.[1]	Somervil, Summerville.
Norvel, de Normanvil ?	Umphravil, de Umphraville.[3]
Ramsay, de Rameseie.	Vans, Vaus, Vaux, de Vaux.
Russell.	Veitch, de Vesci[4] (?)
Ross, Ros, Rose, de Roos.[2]	Vipont, *de veteri ponte.*[5]
Sinclair, de Sancto Claro.	Weir, de Vere.

[1] A great name of old in Teviotdale, now, I suppose, extinct.

[2] Distinguished from the Scotch Rosses by giving the three water-budgets for arms, instead of the Lions of the old Earls of Ross.

[3] I have set down the name of the great Norman barons, who held Redesdale "by the sword," and became Earls of Angus by marriage with the heiress of the old Earls and Marmors, among extant names, because in this, as in so many other instances, the grand old name may lurk unobserved in the misunderstood appellation of some peasant's or burgher's family.

[4] The early seals of the De Vescis, before marshalling arms on shields had become common, have a bunch of *vetches* for a cognizance.

[5] A good old name on the Borders, now, I think, extinct, unless it has taken some humble shape.

Index of Surnames.

—ooo—

"The Old Scots Surnames". Published by Lang Syne Publishers Ltd.,
45 Finnieston Street, Glasgow G3 8JU.
Printed by Dave Barr Print, 45 Finnieston Street, Glasgow G3 8JU.
Reprinted 1994.

ISBN N0. 0 946264 13 9